Introduction 1

Hi, welcome to my:

CW00418205

"a to z guide c   s,
Addiction and Ass

Today is the 6th September 2020, I've had the idea for this a to z guide for a long time.

As you continue through the various introductions to this guide you will notice mention of different dates, the different stages of me coming back to writing this guide.

Part of me thinks I should go back to the beginning and write a proper, single introduction. However, I also think it's worth leaving in the different dates and stages because it sort of sums up the difficulties we have with Mental Health Issues.

I would have loved to of published this guide around the time when I started it back in July 2018. However, as you know as well as I do our world just doesn't work like that, things start then things stop, and then something else catches our attention and so on and so on.

Also between then and now a lot has happened, some good and some bad. Back at the start of 2019 I was very busy with the stuff I was doing at the time as *exboozehound*, in fact I was far too busy. Long story short, after doing far too much in

January and February 2019, I basically fell apart a bit around March 2019. Unfortunately since March 2019 I haven't had a decent period of consistency in which I could concentrate for long enough to re-read my own guide fully to get it ready for publication.

The last time I started to read this guide was the 31st July 2020 and I remember thinking: -

"This is a pile of shite".

Today when I've come back to it again I think it's good and I should get on with it and get it published. I've spent a bit of time looking into and considering trying to get it published in actual on the shelf book form, but as mentioned before I'm finding it difficult to get a period of my life when I'm focused for long enough to do this.

So I've decided to self publish again on Amazon Kindle Direct Publishing as I did with my memoir, still available on Amazon called: -

"enjoy the good and ride out the bad…. exboozehound's thingymajig (First Step Book 1)"

Now I look back at it it's not the snappiest of titles, but neither is the new one.

(If you want to have a look at my first attempt of publishing, go onto Amazon and type in

"exboozehound". I haven't read it since I published it but I'm still proud it has a ✮✮✮✮✮ rating).

Being totally honest I wanted to publish as a physical book because I delusionally imagined the vast amounts of money I was going to make. Being more realistic, and a lot less delusional, a series of short guide's from an unknown like me is never going to make me wealthy.

So when I started reading through this guide again today I decided, like I decided when I started my blog in 2013 and wrote on the *"About Me"* page the last sentence....

"I have had a horrendous time over the last few months and if this blog can help even just one person in a very small way it will be worth it."

(http://www.exboozehound.co.uk/)

And then when I went to upload the e-book on Amazon I saw they now offer an option to create a paperback version of the e-book so it all worked out perfectly, self publish was *definitely* the way to go.

A few people have read the original draft of this a to z guide and given me very positive feedback so I think it's finally time to get it published now, before I talk myself out of it again.

Another reason I wanted to leave the various dates and stages in the final published guide is I wanted to mention the recent few weeks. If you go to YouTube and type in "*exboozehound*" and look on the channel for a vlog called *"When nothings going right…. Go left!"* published on the 30th August 2020 you will be able to see what I said at the time.

We are 7 days on from when I published that vlog, after the 3 week period of horrendous depression I talk about I have had a few days of what I now prefer to call being *"heightened"* rather than using the word *"manic".* Real, at the edge mania is something I've not had for a number of years, but now and then I get a bit too close to mania than I really want to.

I'm hoping with my ramblings so far it's all making total sense and matching with how your life runs, you never know from one day to the next where your state of mind is going to be….

Anyway….

The 3 week low I've just been through has been one of the worst I've been through for a very long time. At times during this low period I was 100% convinced the demons, voices, intrusive thoughts, illness had got me beaten this time. I felt absolutely horrendous with a lot of uncontrollable crying, suicidal thoughts and total and utter physical exhaustion.

If you have Mental Health Issues yourself you will understand this next strange sentence. When I finally broke out of the low period my Mom said to me: -

"It's so fantastic to see you getting better, you look taller….",

It's one of the *many* strange things about Mental Illness, it doesn't just effect you Mentally it effects you physically as well. We shuffle about in a hunched state and can hate what we see in the mirror because what's in the mirror just isn't the real you.

Having been 100% convinced I was beaten this time, and having thoughts like: -

"What's the point in fighting everyday against this illness when the life I have when I'm "well" is pretty shite anyway".

I did come out the other side, like I do every time and deep down I always know I will and I know you will always come out of every bad time to come, now and in the future. How do I know this? You've just got to look at your track record: -

EVERYTIME** you have been in a bad place, no matter how horrendously bad it gets, you have and will continue to come out the other side **EVERY SINGLE TIME! AND I KNOW THIS BECAUSE LIKE ME YOU ARE A WARRIOR AND WARRIORS NEVER GIVE UP!!!!

Introduction 2

Hi, my name is Jon Mansell. I'm also known as *exboozehound*. Long story short I'm a Mentally Ill retired alcoholic, I had a mental breakdown in June 2013, I started a blog in October 2013 (www.exboozehound.co.uk). I have been vlogging on YouTube since June 2016 (www.youtube.com/exboozehound).

I am very proud of what I have achieved since 2013; including helping many people to navigate the sometimes horrendous journey that is Mental Illness, Addiction and Associated Issues....

I think it's worth saying right at the start that my main areas of life experience are Mental Illness and Alcoholism/Addiction but I have spoken with and helped people with many associated issues, including: -

- PTSD
- Self Harm
- Eating Disorders
- OCD
- Anxiety
- Depression
- Adults coping with the fall out of being sexually abused and raped
- Domestic Violence
- Gambling Addiction
- Sex Addiction

Etc, etc....

In this world people are very caught up with being politically correct and to not use certain terms and labels for people coping with many varying issues. I'm not really that big on remaining politically correct, I do sometimes struggle using terms like *"vulnerable people"* but why should I struggle with terms like *"vulnerable people"* when actually I have been one most of my life and still am sometimes....

From the experience I have gained since 2013 and the people I have spoken to I believe that this first set of a to z's you are about to read are relevant to the issues I've listed above any many others.

When someone has survived or is surviving from many issues, we have to reprogram and rebuild ourselves. Whatever that issue might be the process of reprogramming and rebuilding will include what's in this a to z....

I have tried a few times to start writing this a to z guide. I've had this Idea for quite some time now, at the moment I'm still not a hundred percent sure of the title, but it will be something along the lines of....

THE A-2-Z GUIDE OF SURVIVING METAL ILLNESS, ADDICTION AND ASSOCIATED ISSUES

I'm not sure of the title because I'm still not sure how I'm going write it, e.g. from the angle of how *"I survived/survive"* or from the angle of the experience and knowledge I have gained speaking with many people since 2013. Also, should the Mental Illness and Addiction be separate? In my mind the answer to that question is *"NO"* because for me and for many other people it is just two sides of the one story. When I've spoken to people with Mental Illness or Addiction a lot of the stuff we talk about overlaps.

Also I believe that this a to z guide will help people with other issues such as Self Harm, Eating Disorders, PTSD, Anxiety, Depression, OCD and many others....

Today is the 23 July 2018. I'm currently in the middle of a couple of weeks extra medication induced rest. I keep having mini meltdowns and if I'm honest I'm wondering if I am well enough to carry on with the *exboozehound* stuff I've been doing since 2013.

Since late April early May something has changed with my mental wellbeing status. I can't work out just what it is at the moment, my thoughts on the subject today are that since 2013 with everything I've been involved in it has left me mentally, emotionally and physically drained.... The idea of not doing the *exboozehound* stuff scares the ship out of me because if I haven't got that then I become worthless again. I'm pretty sure I will carry on and it's just that the demons are strong at the moment but either way I'm proud of what I've done and achieved up to this point.

A while ago I joked about wanting to write this A 2 Z guide but decided once I'd defined my understanding of A for ACCEPTANCE and B for BAD LEARNED BEHAVIOURS then we didn't need anything else....

Obviously as I've just introduced you to A for ACCEPTANCE and B for BAD LEARNED BEHAVIOURS I will start the guide with these shortly....

But before we get to beginning with A for ACCEPTANCE I want to tell you a little short story:-

I'm currently sitting in Spoons (Wetherspoons) beer yard in Halesowen. It's 13:51; I left the house this morning at 11am and walked the long way to Halesowen, which is about an hour's walk. Whilst I was on that walk, I was doing all I could not to think, at times I was purposely *thinking "MINDFULLY NOTHING"* to stop uncontrollable intrusive thoughts coming into my noggin. Also, whilst on this hour walk I *"double tapped"* many bins, bus stops, telecommunication boxes, etc as I walked past. I then went to the gym for an hour, after the gym I had a pork sandwich sitting by the clock in Halesowen outside a pub known locally as *"Picks"*. A wasp wouldn't leave me alone, wasps don't bother me at all now, and this is because an ex-girlfriend was terrified of wasps. I had to do something about my fear of them, or we would never be able to sit outside in the sun eating lunch or just having a drink in the sun.

Annoyingly the story ends there.... You may not know it but within that crappy story I've covered A for ACCEPTANCE and B for BAD LEARNED BEHAVIOURS....
Some of you will now be thinking: -

"This guy is a tool!"....

I promise you I HAVE covered A for ACCEPTANCE and B for BAD LEARNED BEHAVIOURS and if you continue to read you will work it out for yourself....

Just a quick note on *"working stuff out for yourself"*. Often the stuff we are told to do to help ourselves with our Mental Illness, Addiction and other issues such as PTSD, Anxiety, Depression, Self Harm etc initially make no sense whatsoever. I believe some of what the so-called *"professionals"* tell us to do is purposely ambiguous. I believe this because I *KNOW*, from many years personal experience and from the knowledge I have gained speaking with other people since 2013, that we are *ALL INDIVIDUALS*. And because we *are ALL INDIVIDUALS* we have to take the advice of the professionals and adapt it to fit our *INDIVIDUAL* lives, issues, illnesses and current situations....

I have purposely called this a *"guide"* because that's exactly what it is. It's a guide that may be able to help you point *YOU* in the right direction, what the professionals tell you and what you are about to read aren't rules or must do's set in stone. They are a guide to help *YOU* find *YOUR*

INDIVIDUAL PATH TO RECOVERY AND BEYOND....

Just a little side note on that, advice received from the professionals should probably be followed much more closely than what I've got to say....

Many times in the past people have said to me: -

"Thanks for the Advice"

And my reply to that is usually: -

"Woooooaaaaahhhhhh my words are NOT advice they are just the ramblings of a certified mentalist...."

Introduction 3

So, in the build-up I mentioned it was the 23 July 2018, it is now the 8 November 2018 and I'm trying to write this A 2 Z guide again.

A lot has happened in the last couple of months; a lot of good stuff, someone I've known for a few years has just said to me, in a text: -

"You look well, you look happy".

HAPPY? Until recently this *definitely* isn't how I would of described myself, it is extremely surprising and amazing to feel this way and say I'm *HAPPY* openly....

Hopefully if you follow my guide *YOU* can find some moments of feeling *"Happy"* as well....

Trust me; if it can happen to me, it can happen to *YOU*, if *YOU ARE* willing to put in the effort....

Another thing worth saying before we start the actual A to Z is this first set of A to Z's is purposely short, if you're anything like me you will have the concentration of a gold fish....

It is my hope that you will be able to dip in and out of this guide, pick a random letter and always find something that will make you think differently, not necessarily more positively just more realistically and differently....

Introduction 4

Right, I promise this is the last introduction....

I think if you have got this far you are already doing well and you will have no doubt whatsoever I have some issue's....

My bet is that just like me your thought patterns rarely happen in a linear fashion, they are all over the shop, if you have found the previous introductions frustrating then, good ☺.

Why good?

A life with Mental Illness, Addiction and Associated Issues is frustrating so I like the idea that my a to z guide of navigating Mental Illness, Addiction and Associated Issues is frustrating, because it makes it real....

So finally let get into the "a to z's"....

A - Acceptance

This for me is the keyword to having any chance of making *ANY* progress at all.

Acceptance is a must and not just ***Accepting*** you have an issue or illness once, ***Accepting*** everything that happens, good and bad every day or each hour of that day.

A special lady, Judy X, who I've known for a few years now, who's son John sadly took his own life in 2003, said to me a good while ago now: -

"I know what the difference between you and John is, you accept your illness and John never did which is why he took his own life"....

If you don't find that to be a powerful sentence then you are a bit weird, not that there's anything wrong with being weird....

So, ***Acceptance*** of everything good and bad is your first challenge and not just ***Accepting*** once that you have an illness, ***Accepting*** over and over again, ***Accepting*** something new every single day, every single hour if necessary....

There's a little saying I'm sure you've all heard before....

"It's okay not to be okay"....

Those 6 words are all small words but put them together and you have got something extremely powerful....

Two little sayings I say to myself very regularly will also help you with your **Acceptance** challenge....

"It is what it is"....

And

"Ship hattens"....

Get these three little sayings firmly ensconced in your noggin and work hard on your **Acceptance** and you will have made a huge step forward to your recovery and stability moving forward....

B - Bad Learned Behaviours

Over the years my bet is you will have picked up, cultivated and perfected many **Bad Learned Behaviours**. Automatic negative responses to what life throws at you.

A silly but true example of this is: -

If you bang your hand you will automatically say *"OW"* whether it hurts or not, this is a go to sub conscious *behavioural reaction you have learned*....

This is exactly what we have done over many years, learned and reacted to life with many **Bad Learned Behaviours**, which have helped bring us to the negative place we are currently in.

I believe, with *NO DOUBT WHATSOEVER*, we must purposely and mindfully make the effort to learn how to spot our **Bad Learned Behaviours**, and mindfully work on changing those behaviours to react in a more effective and positive way.

If we are invited to a family thing or a party we will automatically, without any thought, start panicking and worrying days, weeks and maybe months before whatever we've been invited to comes around, this is a **Bad Learned Behaviour**. We have reacted this way for years, so we continue to react this way today as it is a subconscious behavioural pattern.

It is *NOW* time to start spotting those **Bad Learned Behaviours** and start working hard and mindfully on changing them!

WHY? What is the point of stressing, panicking, and worrying about something that hasn't happened yet and won't be happening for a while? The answer to that question is *"There is no point"*, but that doesn't stop us worrying.

So, we must identify our **Bad Learned Behaviours**, and work on reprogramming and rebuilding our noggin's to change these behaviours.

We can't learn to spot and change our **Bad Learned Behaviours** overnight, it takes time and it's not easy, but it is definitely worth the effort!

If you don't believe you can do this then you are wrong!

If I can do it then you can do it too!!!!

C - Change

We can both hate **Change** and love **Change**.

We love **Change** that has a positive effect on our lives. We love **Change** that we don't have to make any effort to make it happen.

We can hate **Change** that involves us making an effort and we hate **Change** that unsettles us....

Fortunately, I've got an example of **Change**, both positive and negative that happened to me recently....

I was in a meeting when I received a phone call/voicemail message to tell me my psychiatrist appointment had been cancelled for the next day, this was of course very negative. I'd been struggling in varying levels for a while but felt able to cope with what I was struggling with, as I knew I was seeing my psychiatrist soon, on the date that had been in my diary for 3 or 4 months.

So all of a sudden I was in a panic and worried about how I would cope without seeing him, as I'd based all of my recent coping mechanisms and strategies around seeing him. I stressed this to the lady who phoned me with the news and asked if there was anything she could do to help.

The next day I got a call saying I'd got another appointment booked in for next week, but it was with someone I didn't know and who didn't know me, but of course I accepted the appointment.

The next week on the way to the new appointment I was concerned about how it would go, I didn't know the stand-in psychiatrist. I was feeling very negative, apprehensive and stressed. Then the time came for the appointment; the new *Changed* appointment and honestly it could not have gone better. It was really good to have a different take on my issues and how to manage them.

The stand-in psychiatrist had a different approach. I thought he went into more detail with what he was telling me. In fact my regular psychiatrist had been more detailed with me at the beginning of our appointments, I was just hearing the same information but from a different person and I was hearing it whilst in a very different state of mind, a very *Changed* state of mind. A *Changed* state of mind I was now in after all the hard work since my mental breakdown in 2013 to keep moving forward with my recovery.

When we can we must embrace Change, because if nothing Changes then we have no chance of continuing our recovery in the right direction.

D - Demons

This could be another D – Difficult....

Recently someone I have spoken to on a number of occasions and met face to face has asked me to explain what the **Demons** are that I speak about a lot.

I think the best I could come up with is....

"We are all individuals and so are our *Demons*".

I know, not hugely helpful!!

I did try a bit harder to help them but like many other things in our lives **Demons** can **Change** and can be anything that affects you negatively like voices, intrusive thoughts, historic issues we bring back up from time to time to beat ourselves with and many more. **Demons** don't just exist in the noggins of us **Mentalists** or addicts it can be something that affects **Normals** as well. Something as simple as them believing their nose is too big and having this thought affects them negatively and could be considered to be a **Demon** for them.

I will come back to trying to explain **Demons** but first I want to look at how we deal with our **Demons** (Black Clouds, Black Dog, Fog etc.).

Like everything else in this world, we have to try to deal with our **Demons** the best way we can, on any given day, or hour. Sometimes it's impossible or seemingly impossible to deal with our **Demons**, if we can't find a positive way around our **Demons** then sometimes I'm afraid we just have to give in to them.

I've got an example from this week: -

On Wednesday I was asleep a lot, I'd tried to get out of bed in the morning but when I stood up, I was dizzy, had blurred vision and a blinding headache. Part of me believes these symptoms were real and part of me believes the symptoms were psychosomatic. Either way I went back to sleep and didn't wake up until about 15.30. When I then very reluctantly got out of bed I wasn't really part of or connected to the day, I just had something to eat and sat in a dark room watching stuff on Netflix.

Going back to **Acceptance**, sometimes we just have to give into our **Demons**. In order to not let my **Demons** do what I know they can and very often seem to enjoy doing to me, I had to **Accept** that my mind body and soul simply needed rest before my **Demons** started telling me how pathetic and worthless I am. I don't think I actually hear voices; I believe it is more I just hear my own negative thoughts put to me by my **Demons**. If I'd had a day like this, sleeping all day, perhaps six months ago it probably wouldn't have only just been one day I wasn't partaking in, it would have been at least two perhaps three days struggling to get back on top of things.

21

Because of the time I've spent and the effort I've put in working hard on reprogramming and rebuilding my noggin since my mental breakdown in 2013 to react in a better way, simply **Accepting** it for what it was, a need for rest, then I'm able to bounce back much quicker.

Reprogramming and rebuilding our noggins is about spotting, questioning and reacting in the right way to those **Bad Learned Behaviours**.

So now I've got to try and go back to explain what my **Demons** are and I'm afraid I can't do much better than what I've said above and what I said to that person in the first place....

"We are all individuals and so are our Demons".

Demons Change, **Demons** are sneaky they pick on your weaknesses and make sure they are constantly finding new issues and weaknesses.

Sometimes I think of my **Demons** as a sort of game we must play, they attack us and we attack back. Or a sort of dance, sometimes we can dance in time with them and sometimes we are completely out of time and one way or another we have to find a way to get back to in time and get some control back.

Another way I see my **Demons** is like buzzing little bees flying all around me whilst I'm wearing a suit of armour. Whilst they are buzzing around me, they find a chink in the armour, a way in and once they've found that chink they are straight in attacking my thoughts in any way possible. We fight back and put the **Demons** back in their place, patch up the chink in the armour and then it starts all over again.

I like to think, every time the **Demons** get the best of me and cause me distress and pain I learn something. I'm not really sure what it is that I learn, apart from every time the **Demons** get hold of me and are too powerful for me, *I beat them sooner or later and knowing they will never beat me into submission is a powerful tool in itself....*

E - "enjoy the good and ride out the bad"

For those of you who don't know me, yet, I came up with this motto of mine years ago; I have it tattooed on my arm.

After I had my mental breakdown life was horrendously painful and very hard going for a while. After a few months when things started to settle down a bit, I started to feel a bit better, I started feeling more connected to life again, I started to feel guilty that things were getting better and I was still signed off work.

Then I realised that if I was going to recover from my mental breakdown things *HAD* to start to settle down. I *HAD* to start feeling a bit better, I *HAD* to start feeling connected to life again, and the guilt I was feeling was a waste of time and energy.

From my experience with Mental Illness and Addiction Issues I'd had most of my life I knew things wouldn't be plain sailing from this point forward, there would definitely be more bad times to get through but hopefully there would be good times again as well. Which is when the motto popped into my noggin:-

"enjoy the good and ride out the bad"

Coming up with my motto and having it tattooed on me made a huge difference to my life and the progress of my recovery. And then when people were quoting it back to me and telling me that my motto helped them as well it was a bit weird, but a good weird.

With Mental Illness and without Mental Illness sometimes life is going to throw hard times at you and when it does you have to find a way through those bad times. You have to fight through those bad times in order to have some good times and when those good times come you must notice them and embrace them.

I know some of you are thinking:-

"I never have good times"

but I'm not talking about days and weeks of good times, I'm talking, *initially*, about fleeting moments when you see something that makes you smile or laugh, fleeting moments when you have a connection with someone or something.

If you start noticing these good moments, I promise you will start having more and more good moments and eventually good hours and good days, maybe even good weeks.

Make sure you remember the good times that you have. We have no problem remembering the bad times, because our **Bad Learned Behaviours** automatically go to the negative memories subconsciously. But we can reprogram and rebuild our noggins to not automatically find bad times in our memories by remembering the good times and building on them.

It's even worth writing them down in a diary to look back on, you *will* start to build a stronger resilience against the bad times and your recovery and the good times can begin again....

Like with **Acceptance** and having to **Accept** things over and over again we must spot and note the good times again and again even the fleeting moments, they can help us fight against all of our negativity....

F - Fix/Fixed

I have spoken to many people since 2013 and quite a few expect something or someone to **Fix** them.

I can tell you categorically: -

There is no one thing or one person that's going to Fix you.

We want to be able to click our fingers and all our issues will go away, that is *NEVER* going to happen.

I've worked very hard to get myself to a place that whatever life throws at me I know 100% I will deal with it one way or another. This hard work makes me very fortunate, I've seen and spoken to so many people that, seemingly, just don't have the capacity to do this, because they want, even expect, someone or something to **Fix** them without putting effort in themselves.

If you are one of those people who don't believe you have the capacity to work hard everyday to move forward with your recovery then you are wrong!

If I can do it you can do it too!!!!

If you are waiting for someone or something to *Fix* you then you have completely the wrong attitude and you must change it *NOW*.

- Meditation isn't gunna *Fix* you....

- Exercise isn't gunna *Fix* you....

- The NHS isn't gunna *Fix* you....

- Mental Health and Addiction professionals aren't gunna *Fix* you....

- I'm not gunna *Fix* you....

- Family and Friends aren't gunna *Fix* you....

- Reiki isn't gunna *Fix* you....

- Alternative therapies aren't gunna *Fix* you....

- Good diet isn't gunna *Fix* you....

- This guide isn't gunna *Fix* you....

I think you might get the point by now, none of these things are going to *Fix* you, but there is a chance a combination off these things and hard work from you will help you, probably not be *Fixed* *(totally),* but able to manage your issues better.

Whether it is right or wrong? I *Accept* I'll never be *Fixed*, but I will manage life and live life rather than just existing and keep learning new ways to help me live life better. I have regular issues, dips and episodes and I try to manage them in the best I can when I can and because I've put the hard work in reprogramming and rebuilding my noggin and **Bad Learned Behaviours**, I can honestly say at times I am *happy* and you can be too.

As I said earlier: -

If you are one of those people who don't believe you have the capacity to work hard everyday to move forward with your recovery then you are wrong!

If I can do it you can do it too!!!!

"...to move forward in our mental health recovery... We must own our own illness & more importantly we must own our own recovery"

exboozehound aka Jon Mansell

G - Gratitude/Grateful

This might seem a bit odd at first, and, to be honest with you I'm cheating with this one. I didn't come to realise myself that **Gratitude** is a very powerful sentiment or feeling and an important word for the successful navigation of Mental Illness, Addiction and Associated Issues. It came from a friend from a long long way away, who I have now met ☺; I also met her 2 sons ☺.

I've taken the below from a Guest Post on the blog called ***"The Evolution Of Awesome Lady"***.... (http://www.exboozehound.co.uk/the-evolution-of-awesome-lady/).

"My defining "light bulb mental health moment" (and I believe we do all eventually have them, so if you are reading this and suffering in some way, please don't lose hope) came the day I realised that the opposite of depression was not happiness! This elusive destination – "happiness" – this abstract state of permanent euphoria that I thought would cure all my woes was not the answer to all the uncomfortable feelings I was experiencing! The opposite of depression, I discovered, was...drum roll... GRATITUDE!! Put simply, stop whinging, find what you do have and be bloody thankful that you have at least that! And it was in explaining this idea to Jon that I gained the nickname "Awesome Lady". If you would like to know more on my thoughts about "gratitude", I am sure that Jon, being the

gentleman he is, might insert a hyperlink back to the blog post he dedicated our conversation about it here. "Gratitude" and "Love" are my mantras these days and have been for a long time now.

(The blog post dedicated to the conversation mentioned above is "Inspirational Words" http://www.exboozehound.co.uk/inspirational-words/).

It may take you a while to get your head around **Gratitude** being the opposite of depression, but I promise you it is worth the effort, have a think....

The cynical might point out the negativity of ignoring destination *happiness,* and what's being suggested is that *happiness* isn't achievable.

A lot of you may consider this to be accurate and for most of my life I would have agreed with you that *happiness* isn't achievable....

I can tell you I was and you are wrong, destination happiness is achievable and the hard work you have to put in to achieve it is very much worth it....

I'm hoping you are able to trust me a little now and believe me when I say: -

"I am, at times, happy".

Again, I'm not saying I'm *happy* for long sustained periods, but I do recognise that, at times, I am able to feel what for many years has been an unachievable and unrecognisable emotion.

Once I learned to recognise and **Accept** this I found it to be very powerful and something *WE* should definitely embrace and note.

And again: -

If I can do this then so can YOU!!!!

When I first found myself using the word *happy* in a text I was pretty blown away about the use of the word and the feelings I could feel. It's out there you just have to work hard to get to know you, your illness and your path to finding some balance for your recovery. But you have to work hard, one day or one hour at a time **Accepting** everything life throws at you along the way and navigating your way through and past it....

H - Hope

The first **H** has to be **Hope** for various reasons. When I set-up my first *exboozehound* peer support group, a men's group, it was, and is, based in an amazing place in Halesowen called *"The Hope Centre"*.

I wanted to start a peer support group and the ladies at the Hope Centre said they would often have men coming into the centre that didn't want to talk to a woman, so it was perfect. They wanted a group for men and I happened to be a man....

I can't remember exactly when the group was first started but I would say it started some time in 2014, and is still going strong, which in itself is quite an achievement as far too many peer support groups fall apart after about 6 to 9 months. The number of people attending the peer support group at The Hope Centre in Halesowen goes up and down, but honestly it's worth doing if just one person turns up.

Hope has to be the first **H** as well because of this simple thing....

Hold

On

Pain

Ends

Don't think I need to say anymore about that....

Hope is important to drive you forward with your recovery, I'm very fortunate that I don't need **Hope** anymore because from the hard work I've put into my recovery instead of **Hope** I have certainty.

I shall now try to explain that....

Whatever comes my way be it a blip, a quick episode or a drawn out bad patch, inside me I always have the certainty that *I WILL* get through it one way or another. Very rarely do I think *"what's the point"*, there's always a point and working hard to get through the blips, episodes and drawn out bad patches is worth it to get back to a good place....

That good place could be a short period of time, a few days where life isn't just an existence, life is living.

That good place could be a single two-second smile or a short giggle.

But when those good times come, long or short, the trick is to remember them no matter what they are.

I used to have a white board behind my television and I once remember writing on the white board a little note about an advert that made me smile and giggle, I have in my mind at the moment the Christmas 2018 Sainsbury's advert it always made me smile....

So from my experience **Hope** can and will take you a long way into your recovery.

I Hope eventually it also brings you to the certainty that I have, because believe me it's an amazing feeling when you get there and I guarantee YOU getting to certainty IS possible, if I can get there so can YOU....

Keep fighting; keep Hoping one day or one hour at a time and YOU WILL get there....

I - Illness

This is where I state the obvious but for some reason it does need stating....

If you have a Mental *Illness* or issues with Addiction and other issues like PTSD, Self-Harm, Eating Disorders etc it is simply an *Illness*, just like any other *Illness*.

Pretty much the whole world insist on specifying between Mental *Illness* and Physical *Illness* but if we take things right back to basics, if Mental *Illness* is down to a chemical imbalance in your head then why is it not a Physical *Illness*?

Unless I'm an alien I would imagine just like me your head is connected to your body by a something called a neck. Your head is part of your body, part of your Physical being; therefore any Mental *Illness* is also a Physical *Illness*.

There are many theories as to what happens to us as Addicts, but: -

- If your drug of choice is booze you drink it and it goes into your physical body

- If your drug of choice is cocaine it usually goes up your nose again effecting and entering your physical body.

I could go on, in fact I'm going to go on with just one more example: -

- If your Addiction is gambling you put your bets on and you are happy or sad about the results, the feelings of happiness or sadness yet again manifest in your physical body....

There are many people in the world that have a Mental *Illness* or a Physical *Illness*, to make things simpler all we have to do is get rid of two words, Mental and Physical. Once we have removed these words we are simply left with the word *Illness* and be you a mentalist, Addict or have other Associated Issues you simply have an *Illness*.... *FACT!!!!*

While we are stating the obvious, if we are struggling with Mental *Illness*, Addiction and Associated Issues then we simply have an *Illness*. Yes it can and will make our lives horrendous at times but taking it right back to basics it's just an *Illness*. We need to address the fact that people often hide for far too long behind the *Illness* label. It's ok to hide behind this label for a short while but in order to move forward with your recovery from that *Illness* you have to step out from behind the reasons and excuses and fight back, try everything you can to find what works for you....

"In order to move forward with our recovery we must own our Illness and more importantly own our recovery...."

J - Judgement

I have to start **J** for **Judgement** off with one of those sayings, there are many versions of this saying, and I've just picked this one off the web....

"Before you start to judge me, step into my shoes and walk the life I'm living and if you get as far as I am, just maybe you will see how strong I am".

Over the years I have done many things and acted in ways that I have been **Judged** for because of my Mental Illness and Addiction.

Even though I have been soba since 2003, I'm aware that people still **Judge** me based on the way I behaved when I was still drinking.

To be honest I still **Judge** me on the way I behaved and some of the horrible, out of order, embarrassing things I did when I drank, some of them will never go away, some of them still make me shudder with shame when I think of them.

In the main I have moved on but sometimes I think it's not a bad thing to have these thoughts as they may well be one of the reasons I have remained soba. Staying soba since 2003 has not been easy, still to this day I miss booze, but what I definitely don't miss is waking up the next day and having know Idea what I did the night or the couple of days before....

Anyway, back to knowing that some people still **Judge** me based on the way I behaved when I was still drinking….

They are now **Judging** me on things that happened maybe twenty plus years ago, I don't actually have an issue with this, I don't expect people to trust me.

Many times when speaking to someone who stopped drinking or drugging only a few weeks or a month ago, automatically they believe that being soba for a short time means friends and family should trust them again, based on what?

- Every time you have let them down over the years

- Every time you've said *"this time it's for real"*

In order for your friends, family and loved ones to trust you, *YOU* have to keep proving they *CAN* trust you every single day.

We should never expect the trust to happen overnight, it just doesn't work that way! And you expecting that trust isn't going to do you any favours in the long run. Like me you may spend the rest of your life being **Judged** for your Addiction and your behaviour whilst in the depths of that Addiction, that's just the way it is. But as I said earlier I still **Judge** me for my Addiction and the things I did and you may well also for many years to come, but eventually you will be able to put most or all of these things behind you. The reason I've gone on a bit on this subject is I know I spent many years using my own **Judgement** of me as a perfect excuse to carry on or start drinking again and I've seen quite a few addicts do exactly the same.

You have to get this straight in your head, **Judgement** of you and the lack of trust people have in you are not reasons or excuses to continue with your Addiction, if you are going to play that game things are not going to **Change**.

Going right back to the start of this guide, to **Acceptance**, you have to **Accept** the possibility of being **Judged** and mistrusted for a long time to come and simply tackle your Addiction issues, and I know you will of heard this before, **ONE DAY AT A TIME....**

And to the friends, family and loved ones of those with Addiction issues although I believe you have a right to **Judge** and not trust the person with Addiction issues you have to find a way to understand that addiction is an **Illness**.

Many times I have spoken to people close to those with Addiction Issues and many times I have heard:-

"All they have to do is promise me they will never do it again".

I'm afraid this is a promise those of us with Addiction Issues can't actually make, I've been soba since 2003 and I still can't make this promise.

Although I still can't make this promise as time goes on it is more likely I will not go back to my old ways. But even all these years on that phrase that you will of also heard many times before, it still has to be done **ONE DAY AT A TIME....**

We also very much and often get **Judged** for having a Mental **Illness** an **Illness** that no one can actually see. I don't have an issue with this either....

Rather than wasting energy worrying about people **Judging** you and your **Illness** use that energy to work hard on keeping moving forward with your management of your **Illness**. Find that strength and determination inside you and once you've found it show those around you just how strong and determined you are, again and again and again....

It used to annoy me when depression and Mental Illness was likened to diabetes all the time. But now I know a bit more about it, as my nephew was diagnosed with Type 1 diabetes at a very young age, just like all **Illnesses**, you have to take the right medication and do the right things. Often people with diabetes will be **Judged** as well, **Judged** wrongly about the lifestyle they led that caused their diabetes.
Like with Mental Illness and Addiction people, often wrongly, make the assumption that something must have happened to make you this way. Don't get me wrong I do believe that traumas, circumstances and situations can bring on Mental illness and Addiction almost like it switches a switch in you. However, I

also believe, well *know* that it's not always the case. Like any other **Illness** there can be something inside a person that means they are more inclined to go down certain paths to Mental Illness, Addiction and Associated Issues like Anxiety, OCD, PTSD etc.

Chances are you disagree with me and that's fine.

I've worked extremely hard to get to a place that the **Why's** don't matter, *Why* waste your energy on *Why?* You are where you are and now you should use that energy on moving forward and finding ways to manage everything life throws at you, *NOT* worrying and wasting your time and energy on *Why?*

As long as you are honest with you and can say: -

*"I'm doing all I can to understand me and move forward with my **Illness**"*

Then who gives a poop if someone is **Judging** you...? **Not me that's for sure!!!!**

And if someone is **Judging** you, the way I like to look at it is that's their problem, Mental Illness, Addiction and Associated Issues are real, some people **Judge** us because they don't' believe we have an actual **Illness**....

....They are WRONG and they are MORONS!!!!

I might have gone on a little bit more than I'd planned to with *J for Judgement*. I seem to of also introduced a lot about **Trust**, I'm not even convinced **Judgement** and **Trust** are words that are semantically talked about together but it just felt right when I was going through this a to z for the last time before publishing. *(I'm also not sure about the word semantically but I'm going with that as well....)*

So to finish lets go right back to the start of *J for Judgement....*

"Before you start to judge me, step into my shoes and walk the life I'm living and if you get as far as I am, just maybe you will see how strong I am".

You will be **Judged,** You will be mistrusted, and only *YOU* can change that.

It might take a long time; it might be that some people never change their opinion of you....

But....

As long as YOU are honest with YOU and can say "I'm doing all I can to understand me and move forward with my Illness"

Then who gives a poop if someone is Judging YOU...?

Not me that's for sure!!!!

K - Keep Going

Or more precisely "Keep going ;)"....

"Keep going" and **"Keep on Keeping on"** are phrases I would guess you have used and/or heard many times and absolutely you do have to **Keep going** whatever comes your way, you have to keep fighting and striving to move forward.

The reason I wrote: -

"Or more precisely **"Keep going ;)"**...."

Is when I started the blog I would finish every page and post with: -

"Keep smiling ☺ *".*

Until I realised that in using *"Keep smiling* ☺ *".* I was encouraging myself and others to *"Keep smiling* ☺ *",* no matter what. The problem with that is if you keep smiling no matter what you will sometimes be covering your true feelings with a fake smile which is a waste of energy. You need to be using that energy to fight for your recovery not to make people around you happier and more comfortable.

Yes, of course, sometimes you do have to smile things off, people have to do this all the time whether they have an *Illness* or not, Mental or

Physical. But sometimes you have to **Accept** what is going on is something that can't be or is very difficult to smile off.

At these times you have to: -

"It's okay not to be okay"

And do what your body and mind is telling you to do. Give in a bit and rest and recuperate, just like every other person on the planet with or without Mental Illness, Addiction and Associated Issues, resting helps you bounce back quicker....

So, **Keep going** one day or one hour at a time, **Accept** whatever comes your way and react the best way possible to help you to continue *"Keep on Keeping on"*....

Keep going ;)

I feel there is a lot more I could write about **Keep going**, but sometimes it's important to keep things as simple as possible and, *hopefully*, what's in the rest of this a to z guide is going to help you do what *YOU* need to do to **Keep going.**

L - Living Life

Far too often we are just existing; this can be one of the difficult effects of **Living Life** one day or one hour at a time. You can end up not connected to the world and the people around you; all you're doing is existing to get from one bad patch to the next and just existing in between.

Even if things seem to be going okay for you you're thinking about when it will all go wrong again and when it does go wrong the just existing starts all over again.

I'm very fortunate, through all the effort I've made to keep fighting against the **Illness**, the **Demons**, all the blips, episodes and longer periods of being low, stressed, horrendously depressed and suicidal thoughts, I finally feel like I'm **Living Life**. Not all the time but enough of the time to give me a buzz, a smile, a feeling of *happiness* and believe me that is achievable and very much worth all the effort.

To be able to use the word *happy* and have feelings of *happiness* is extremely special, amazingly rewarding and something you will want to keep working hard to achieve....

Living Life and feeling *happiness* is bloody awesome!!!! *(I'm smiling now just writing that, wow!!!!)*

Yesterday (19th September 2018) for many reasons was a bostin day!!!!

The sort of day that makes all the horrendous pain we fight through on a daily basis worth it....

You may not believe those sort of days exist but if I can have a day like that then *you can too*, just gotta keep fighting one day at a time....

" *enjoy the good and ride out the bad* "

exboozehound September 2018

If all we can do at this current time is exist then that's what we have to **Accept**, that's what we have to do, take each day our each hour one at a time and keep fighting to get through and come out of the other side.

This is what I still do on a regular basis, sometimes I guess my life could be described, as a *"White Knuckle Ride"* and I'm pretty sure your life is the same at times. You may even feel that your life is *ALWAYS* like this and I understand that, I promise you I do, BUT we have to exist and keep fighting in order to get to start **Living Life** again....

As the saying goes: -

"You've got to be in it to win it"....

Many of you may believe this will never be the case for you, you will only ever exist and never really *Live Life* again, But, and I think I may of said a few times in this a to z guide....

If I can do this then I GUARANTEE YOU CAN TOO!!!!

- Keep existing....

- *Keep Going....*

- Keep fighting…

- Keep working hard on YOUR recovery....

And you will eventually start Living Life again, I promise you!!!!

M - Madness

Those of you who have known me for a while will probably of expected **M** to be **Mentalist** but we'll come back another time to that one on the next **M**....

"M for Madness" I think is important and that's why I've made it the first **"M"**.

Yes **Madness** is a very politically incorrect word, I still use it all the time and much worse politically incorrect words and phrases, because they are only words and often the politically incorrect words sum things up much better.

It's an important word to look at a bit closer. Many of you or maybe all of you will of thought yourself to be **Mad,** or perhaps **"Mad** *as a bucket of frogs"*, again not a very politically correct saying.. Maybe some of you are **Mad** but even if you are **Mad** it's still possible to live your life and enjoy life rather than just existing and just going from one **Mad** episode to another.

The reason I believe **Madness** is such an important word to look at is it's very often a go to answer to the questions like....

"How do you feel right now?"

Answer

"I feel like I'm going *Mad* "

Or

"Everything in the world seems *Mad* to me"

Or

Many other answers including the often, go to words to describe Mental Illness, Addiction and Associated Issues, *Mad* or *Madness*.

Also when you're sitting there and you are....

- Struggling to concentrate....

- You don't want to go anywhere....

- You don't want to see anyone....

- You can't answer your phone....

- You can't phone anyone for help....

- You haven't seen or spoken to another person for 3 days....

- You can't be bothered to eat....

And all you want to do is....

- Drink....

- Take drugs *(prescribed or not)*....

- Self harm....

- Plan how you are going to take your own life....

etc, etc to stop the unexplainable

- Voices....

- ***Demons***....

- Intrusive thoughts....

- Absolute hatred for yourself and the life you live....

- Total pointlessness of life going from one episode to the next, just existing in between....

How else can you explain this other than **Madness**?

You can even look in the dictionary for the word **Madness**....

madness

/ˈmadnəs/

noun

the state of having a serious mental illness
"in his madness he destroyed the work of years"

Similar: (insanity) (insaneness) (dementia) (mental illness) (derangement) (⌄)

So, even if the words *Mad* and *Madness* are politically incorrect having a Mental Illness is defined in the dictionary by using these words....

I've spoken to many people who have told me and insisted to me they are *Mad* and nine times out of ten they're not *Mad* they're just muddled and need some help to unravel their perceived *Madness*.

They've been struggling with what's going on in their noggins, without speaking to anyone about it, for so long that now nothing seems to make any sense anymore. Therefore the "I'm *Mad* ", "I'm going *Mad* " starts to bounce around your noggin and if you do nothing about it inevitably it just continues to get worse and more and more real.

When things get out of hand for me my *Demons*, still to this day enjoy telling me....

"Your Mad"....

And....

"This time the *Madness* is going to consume you and destroy you"....

I have to be honest and tell you sometimes I believe the *Demons*. But because of the hard work I've put into my recovery for years, these days I don't believe them for very long. Sometimes I fight back straight away and other times I have to give into them, knowing they're wrong, and get some rest to recharge the batteries to keep fighting back against the little sneaky **Demon** bastards.

If you think you're **Mad** don't allow that thought to fester and get out of control, get some help, talk to someone, go and see your GP, find out if you have a self referral Mental Health service in your area. Whatever you do, do something; doing nothing means things will only get worse.

I've spoken with many people who have told me: -

*"You can't help me I'm **Mad** "*

And very quickly and usually relatively easily we can start to un-pick whatever it is that makes them believe they are *"**Mad** as a bucket of frogs"*....

So, talk to someone, be **Open** and honest with whoever you can, perceived **Madness** can easily get out of hand and once it is out of hand it will be a lot harder to come back from.

If you are reading this with the belief you are Mad do something about it NOW and things will start to get better, not overnight, but bit by bit you will come to Accept you are NOT Mad you just need help with your Illness....

N - NHS

How could the first *"N"* not be *NHS*?

(Weirdly as I'm writing this I'm currently sitting in Russell's Hall Hospital waiting for my number "B15" to pop up on a screen to get some blood tests, the screen is currently on "3" so shouldn't be long...).

What can I say about the *NHS?...*

My bet is you are sitting there thinking: -

"He's gunna go on for pages and pages slagging off the NHS now?"

Well, the first thing I will say about the *NHS* is we are extremely lucky to have a *National Health Service* and we should support it as much as we possibly can....

You weren't expecting that were you?...

The second thing I will say about the *NHS* is after my mental breakdown in June 2013, if I'd left my recovery to the *NHS* and waited for them for *Fix* me, I'm pretty sure I'd be dead right now....

Initially the *NHS* we're totally and utterly useless and if anything they and the *"system"* made my situation much worse, they made me more *Ill*. And unfortunately this is still happening *FAR TOO OFTEN!!!!* Rather than helping me recover quickly and get back to *"normal"* life I waited and waited for help but none came....

I won't go into the details here but there is a post on my blog called ***"You need therapy the queue is 2 months"....***

I think you'll agree the first and second things I've said about the **NHS** don't exactly support and compliment each other. But here's the thing, since my mental breakdown in 2013, when I started to get back on my feet I was very angry, which is one of the things that brought me to starting the blog. I shouted loud and I shouted publicly, and I started speaking with senior management at the **NHS** and CCG (Clinical Commissioning Group).

Going to many meetings with them and other organisations like Adult Social Care, local Councils, Police, MP's and other front line organisations and people. I can honestly say I can see things getting better. If they're not getting better where you are and for you personally, please trust me when I tell you the powers that be, in the main, are genuinely doing all they can to make things better for everyone for both patients and staff. I hope you can trust me on that?

However, for me this genuine want for things to get better is moving far to slowly, because everything has to go through many meetings, many committees and reels and reels of red tape, ***so if your reading this and you are that senior management my message to you is "FFS strap*** *a pair on and make those changes happen now, not in X number of years, NOW!!!!"*.

Of course, in the time I've been involved with the senior management and other people within the **NHS** and other establishment organisations and people I've heard it said many many times….

"We just don't have the funding"….

I'm afraid this is no longer an excuse that can and should be allowed to be used, the funding hasn't been available now for a long time and like any other business or organisation the **NHS** has to adapt and change to the current climate. As I said earlier *"we are extremely lucky to have a **National Health Service** and we should support it as much as we possibly can"*. However I'm now going to say something that on the surface is utterly ridiculous but also true….

If the NHS was a factory, call centre, shop or any other business or organisation it would have been closed down years ago….

As I said *"I'm now going to say something that on the surface is utterly ridiculous but also true…."* I have said this many times to many people and no one has ever disagreed with me, however ridiculous it sounds. If we had an endless pot of cash the current *"system"* could not be fixed. It's not money that's needed to make things better it's the people who work within the **NHS** and those of us that use and need it working together in a better way, working as a team.

The **NHS** is *OUR* **National Health Service** it belongs to and is run for *US* and *OUR* country, It is all of our responsibilities to make it the best **National Health Service** it can possibly be. There has to be a **Change** of attitude and approach of those in charge who can make a difference, they need to start by **"Strapping on a pair"** and *really actually* making a difference.

Changes must happen *NOW* for many reasons, including something that was in the news this morning about a 16 year old boy who raped and killed a 14 year old girl, obviously very shocking and horrendous news. But when I was watching that news story do you want to know what I was waiting for? Yup, you guessed it the sentence....

"He was being seen by mental health services".

We hear this far too often in relation to horrible crimes committed. **That young girl would still be alive if we had the mental health service we should have, sorry but it's true....**

The money isn't available, get used to it, more has to be done with less money, get used to it, if I hear *"we just don't have the funding"* again there's a possibility I'm going to start swearing, get used to it.

The **NHS** has to get used to doing more with less.... **But here's the thing they can't do it on** *their own, WE have to help them make it happen and we can do this in many ways....*

First of all don't expect the **NHS** to **Fix** you that's *NEVER* going to happen....

I've seen far too often when people get appointments for therapy or new medication they get excited and think this is the start of their recovery. Yes it could well be the starting point but the **NHS** isn't going to **Fix** you. You have to put in a lot of hard work and effort.

So many times I've seen people give up when they realise they've actually got to do stuff for themselves and make an actual effort to keep doing the right things. Mental Illness, Addiction and Associated Issues don't get better overnight they take a long time and a lot of hard work and effort, time, hard work and effort *YOU* have to put in which is not easy, **but I promise you it's worth it....**

And again, If I can do it then YOU can too!!!!

Something else I've seen far too often is people telling me they get no support whatsoever from the **NHS** or GP.

Just to clarify the way I understand it is there are basically two areas of care within the **NHS** and Mental Health, Primary Care and Secondary Care. Basically if you're seeing your GP or maybe a councillor you are in Primary Care and if you're seeing a Mental Health worker, psychologist or psychiatrist you are in Secondary Care.

When people tell me they are getting no support whatsoever from the **NHS** or GP, my first question will usually be: -

"When did you last see a mental health care professional or your GP?"

Yes, sometimes it is the **NHS's** or GP's fault that people are not receiving the support they should. Quite often people fall into a *"no mans land"* between Primary and Secondary care. However, far too often people will tell me: -

"I missed an appointment and ignored a few letters".

If you do this, even if you're in secondary care you could end up being taken of the list and referred back to your GP. It is very unlikely your GP will chase you up, apart from maybe a yearly Mental Health Review. And once **NHS** secondary care has sent a couple of letters, usually including one advising you have been referred back to your GP as they haven't heard from you, they won't be chasing you up either, so your recovery and getting back onto your recovery path is now your responsibility....

As I've said before....

"....to move forward in our mental health recovery.... We must own our own illness & more importantly we must own our own recovery"

exboozehound aka Jon Mansell

I might be sounding a bit heartless hear, I don't mean to, I completely understand a person with Mental Illness, Addiction and Associated Issues will often not have the capacity to fight their own corner. If you can't fight your own corner at the moment *YOU MUST* find someone to help you, *YOU MUST* reach out for support, keeping your recovery on track yourself is very very difficult, don't try to do it on your own....

The last thing for now on the **NHS** is as I said before....

*"They won't **Fix** you"*.

Not a single thing on its own will. The support people like me and third party organisations can offer can make a huge difference. I have no problem in saying I believe that this support may well be more effective than what the **NHS** can offer *BUT* support not from the **NHS** must be in addition to what the **NHS** has to offer.

I've met many people who start to feel better after receiving support outside what the **NHS** is doing with them and because they are feeling better they stop taking their medication and stop going to **NHS** appointments. This is *NOT* how it works; third party organisation support has to run along side what the **NHS** can do for you. Third party organisations and other individuals and treatments, such as Reiki and other alternative medicine compliment what the **NHS** does and definitely don't and never will replace what the **NHS** does....

I said earlier that the **NHS** has to change its attitude, this isn't a one way street, *WE* have to change out attitude as well and *WE* have to work with the **NHS** with a better attitude.

It is difficult to explain what I mean here but think about this, if you sit down in a restaurant and say to the waiter or waitress....

"The mixed grill, make sure you cook it properly because the last one I had was pretty crap and make sure you bring it to my table with a smile, now run along and make that happen"....

If they haven't thrown you out at this point, what sort of service do you think you are likely to get?

We all have to work together to make the **NHS**, the **National Health Service** we are very lucky to have work better for everyone.

No, they are not perfect and are never likely to be but neither are we….

*"**Them** and **Us** doesn't work"*….

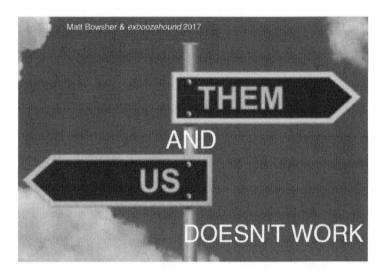

O - Open

My noggin is telling me there are many ways we can use the word **Open** to help us navigate the world of Mental Illness, Addiction and Associated Issues. But at the moment I can only think of two: -

*"**Open** and Honest"....*

And

*"You have to be **Open** to new things, good, bad and ugly"....*

"**Open** and Honest" - without wishing to caption the obvious, in order to move forward in any recovery, whatever the issues, you have to be **Open** and Honest, with other people and even more importantly with yourself.

With the blogging, vlogging and many meetings I've done as *exboozehound*, I think I might be a little too **Open** and Honest at times. But being **Open** with those around you, friends, family, colleagues, your GP, your Mental Health professional, your Addiction professional and many other people and organisations, including the Police, is very important.

Sometimes unfortunately being **Open** can cause stress to those around us. I have an example from this morning: -

I'm off into Birmingham for something and if I'm honest, and we know I am, the thought of it has been stressing me out. I've just parked my car at my Moms and I'm now on the number 9 bus writing this. I knocked on Moms door just to tell her I was leaving my car there to go into Birmingham and she could see instantly I was stressed, which inevitably leads to Mom being stressed about me. Whilst waiting for the bus I've sent Mom a text saying: -

"I'll be ok once I calm down a bit".

And now I'm on the bus and a much calmer I've sent Mom another text saying: -

"I'm on the bus, much calmer".

Some of you might be thinking *"how pathetic"* and you could be right. However because I'm **Open** about everything, including things that can be considered to make me look pathetic, I know I'll handle going into Birmingham no problems at all and in part this comes from simply expressing, however briefly, that I am a bit stressed....

We must find the strength to be **Open** with GP's, health care professionals and the Police, but I know many people who aren't **Open**, including me. I was never fully **Open** with my GP, in part because I didn't want to be labelled **Mad** or Mentally Ill. I knew for many years I was more ill than *"anxiety and depression"*, but I thought if I was labelled *"Mentally Ill"* I'd lose my job, house, girlfriend etc and you know what in a way I was right.

If I'd been more **Open** I might still be taking part in everyday, normal life. But because I wasn't as **Open** as I should of been I ended up having my mental breakdown, which I can tell you takes *A LOT* of effort, commitment, pain, stress, anxiety and extremely hard work to come back from.

As a result of my mental breakdown me trying to avoid losing my job, house and girlfriend etc happened anyway. I'm definitely **Open** now with my healthcare professionals, I have to be to stand a chance and if I do need extra help at any time I'm **Open** about it and seek professional help. The quicker you are **Open** and ask for help the more chance you've got at getting through whatever's going on quicker and the quicker you get through your current pain the less damage it does.

Yes you are right; I did say earlier we have to be honest with the Police, not with things like walking up to a rozzer and saying....

"Hi, earlier on today I was doing 72mph in a 60 zone...."

If you encounter the Police along the way when you're having problems with your Mental Illness, Addiction and Associated Issues be honest with them about what's really going on. Yes you might be drunk as a skunk and possibly misbehaving, but if you tell the Police you have issues and need some help, they can help you if they have all the relevant information and can point you in the right direction or refer you to a specialist team.

From the meetings I've been to with quite a few Police officers, some of them very senior ranks, I can tell you with my hand on my heart there are many rozzers out there that will do everything they can not to criminalise your actions and behaviour.

Of course not all rozzers are this way inclined but what have you got to lose? I was never that keen on the Police when I was still drinking, but why would I be, they kept arresting me and ruining my night. But I can tell you that I've seen with my own eyes the compassion many Police officers have with those of us that may need a little help and the passion to make sure they treat us with dignity and respect. If you just carry on drunkenly mouthing off and swearing at the Police inevitably you will be arrested for drunk and disorderly.
(*That's what I've been told anyway....*)

I've got a couple of emails from senior Police officers stuck to the wall above my desk, I noticed yesterday that on both of them under their name, rank and contact details it says....

"Preventing crime, protecting the public and helping those in need"

Years ago I would of laughed at this and said *"yeah right...."* but now through spending time with Police officers of all different ranks I know this to be true. They're not just there to stop your fun, ruin your night, annoy you and arrest you they are genuinely there to help people in need. The Police are as *front line* as it gets, if you see someone behaving oddly you don't call the Fire or Ambulance Service you call the Police.

With the Police being the front line inevitably they will be called first and often arrive at very difficult situations not knowing if the people in those situations are struggling with their Mental Health, Addiction and Associated Issues. So it is imperative that the Police get their approach right, approaching people as an individual who possibly needs their help and compassion rather than approaching people heavy handed just to arrest them.

I've seen both approaches and the first approach definitely has a better outcome, so we must support our Police officers in the same way as we must support the **NHS** and where we can make their jobs easier. We *MUST* work together to make the current situation better because....

"Them and Us doesn't work...."

"**Open** to new things good, bad and ugly" - these new things could be many different things, medication, coping mechanisms, triggers, alternative therapy, exercise, eating better, etc, etc. If you're not **Open** to new possibilities and new ways to help you keep your recovery moving forward then your recovery will be much harder....

A quick example....

I used to hate it when people always wanted to talk about *triggers* and *coping mechanisms* but eventually I got why people thought them to be so important. Whilst I can finally agree it is definitely worthwhile keeping an eye out for *triggers* and *coping mechanisms*, they are like everything else in this world that never makes any sense, they are changeable and adaptable. If you don't **Accept** the changeability and are unwilling to adapt, again your recovery will be much harder....

The example: -

I'd lay money on every one of you at some point being told: -

"You should go for a walk and get some fresh air, it'll make you feel much better"....

This is utter bollox *and* completely true at the same time. I do a lot of walking but a while back walking was a trigger for me, more of a trigger than a coping mechanism. I'd walked into Halesowen, about a 25-minute walk, I was walking through the bus station and spotted and heard two or three women chatting and laughing, my noggin convinced me that they knew I was mentally ill and they were laughing at me. I became very paranoid and immediately turned around to walk home, the walk home was tortuous because now not only were those three women laughing at me it felt like everyone was staring at me, everyone knew I was mentally ill and they were **Judging** me. As I turned into my road I started crying uncontrollably and by the time I got to the front door I was a complete mess....

So the moral of the story/example, just because something once helped you cope with your issues and indeed currently helps you deal with your issues that doesn't necessarily mean it will *ALWAYS* be an effective coping mechanism. You have to **Accept** the changeability and be willing to adapt again and again and again....

So you *HAVE* to be **Open** to **Accepting** and finding new ways to navigate your recovery to enable you to start to **live your life** rather than just existing....

P - Patience

The first **P** word that popped into my head was *Perspective* but I'll come back to that one as I think **Patience** is a much more important and powerful word....

I'm going to state the obvious again, but if you have Mental Illness, Addiction and Associated Issues in your life, **THEY WILL NOT GET BETTER OVER NIGHT**. This for me is one of the things that makes a recovery that keeps moving forward something very difficult Ney seemingly impossible to find.

Recovery definitely isn't a linear phenomenon you will *HAVE* to get used to moving forward three steps and then falling back two. Sometimes falling back four steps and when this happens finding a way to pick yourself up, dust yourself off and start all over again. This will happen many many times, many many soul destroying times but I promise you if you can find the **Patience** within you and the belief that things can and will get better then they will get better.

When I had my mental breakdown and ten years prior to that got off the booze I didn't believe I could ever bounce back from the mental breakdown or stay off booze but with a lot of effort, **Patience**, hard work and sporadic belief, my recovery continues to move forward.

I wish I could find and use some simple numbers and statistics to describe and quantify how much of the time my recovery is moving forward, how much of the time my recovery is sitting still and how much of the time my recovery is going backwards but I can't.

However, what I can say for sure is compared to even just a year ago I am more often *"enjoying the good"* and much better equipped to *"ride out the bad"* and two years ago I never thought that would be possible....

So again if you trust me, even if only in a very small way then trust me, what I've achieved in my recovery is achievable in *YOUR* recovery. *YOUR* recovery is going to need a lot of **Patience**, if you can find that **Patience** then even though you will inevitably often move three steps forward and then four steps back you will learn to **Accept** this is.

Once you have **Accepted** finding **Patience** and staying **Patient** is very important, which is extremely difficult and almost impossible at times, then you have another very powerful tool to better navigate your world with Mental Illness, Addiction and Associated Issues.

Q - Questions

What other word could **Q** be?

There are not many options for **Q**, in fact I think I'm going to have to make some **Q** words up with the next a to z guides....

Questions are both good and bad, you asking **Questions** is both good and bad, people asking **Questions** is both good and bad. All these options are both good and bad depending on the mood you are in and the timing.

I had to apologise to someone the other day, I'd given them a call to see how they were and they wouldn't stop asking me **Question** after **Question.** I tried counting to ten because my annoyance levels wasn't their fault, I had been grumpy most of the morning, but unfortunately my eventual reaction wasn't the best, basically I said *"I couldn't be arsed to talk"* and hung up....

At times if I was actually able to write down every single **Question** that popped into my poorly wired noggin throughout the day I would of written something a kin in length to War and Peace.

Sometimes I knew my noggin was asking **Questions** of me without knowing what the **Questions** being asked actually were. I would **Question** every single decision and why I was having to make that decision and also **Question** the **Questions** I was asking about the **Questions**. I didn't actually know what the **Questions** were....

A bit confusing? Well that's how my noggin is all day sometimes or for days at a time, always some activity going on, being unable to work out what the point of that activity was and why so many unanswerable unimportant **Questions**. That's what life is like with Mental Illness, Addiction and Associated Issues, nothing actually makes any sense and woe betide that you try to make any sense of it.... Good luck with that one!!!!

exboozehound 2017

"The only thing you can guarantee with mental illness is nothing ever makes sense, FACT!!!!"

I'm pretty sure the **Q** entry in this a to z guide has left you with many more **Questions** than you started with. Believe it or not this is both good and bad, we can spend the rest of our lives asking **Question** after **Question** or we can find a way only to ask the **Questions** we must.

We could ask the **Question** *"what are the lottery numbers going to be this Saturday?"* And if someone could answer that for us that would be a very lucrative and worthwhile **Question** but if we change that **Question** just a smidge it becomes totally pointless, let me prove this for you.

New **Question**, *"what we're the lottery numbers last Saturday?"*

The **Question** is now utterly pointless unless we have a time machine, I've only changed the **Question** very slightly, and this is what I've had to do with many many **Questions** over the years to allow my recovery to keep moving forward.

Another couple of contradictory things have just popped into my noggin. I mention contradictory as I know I contradict myself all the time. This comes from my belief that pretty much everything that life throws at us can be considered both positive and negative and whether something is positive or negative doesn't really matter, what matters is how we react to the situation that counts....

With that in mind....

Sometimes we must ask others and ourselves **Questions** that we really don't want and probably can't handle the answers to. Other times we absolutely shouldn't ask **Questions** that we really don't want and probably can't handle the answers to. Although that initially makes no sense whatsoever, like so much else I say, you will either already know exactly what I'm going on about or if you give it a little thought you will understand it very soon. If you don't understand it at all and you're thinking....

"Deep down this exboozehound guy is a bit of a moron"....

That's fair enough.

Hopefully this ambiguous **Questions** entry in this a to z guide will help you find a way to know what **Questions** are helpful and productive and which **Questions** aren't.

Or it may just simply confuse you, like it has me as I've read this back, I haven't altered it as I believe it must of made some sort of sense when I first wrote it....

R - Rest

At first when you look at the fact I've decided to put **Rest** as the first **R** I'm betting a number of you are thinking....

"Lazy git, he's putting no effort into this whatsoever"

Well you couldn't be more wrong....

I was going to do *R for Relationships* but I thought that to be too obvious so I thought of another **R** and **Rest** is what I came up with.

As obvious and seemingly unimaginative as it seems this is a very very important word in helping us navigate the world of Mental Illness, Addiction and Associated Issues....

I will be stating the obvious in the following....

For many years I heard the same sentence over and over again and I'm betting you will of heard this sentence many times as well....

"What are your Triggers and what coping mechanisms do you have in place?"....

My reaction to this until fairly recently was, well unrepeatable in civilised society. However when I finally did get an understanding of what my *Triggers* and *Coping Mechanisms* where I was able to stop swearing at anyone who used the words *trigger* and *coping mechanisms* in my presence.

I had a *triggers* and *coping mechanisms* epiphany moment and the epiphany was based around the *FACT* that *triggers* and *coping mechanisms* are fluid, they **Change** all the time.

Going back right to the start, **A** for **Acceptance**, once you can **Accept** that your *triggers* and *coping mechanisms* are fluid and can **Change** from day to day or hour to hour then you're getting there.

You are starting to understand YOU and what YOU need to do to build YOUR recovery....

You will now be thinking....

"WTF? He's said **R** *is for* **Rest** *and then not mentioned it at all"....*

Well although **Rest** might of seemed lazy and unimaginative it absolutely isn't because **Rest** is as important to me and my continuing recovery as *ANYTHING* else that I have to do to try and keep my recovery on track.

If I get tired I get ill it's as simple as that and unlike pretty much everything else around the *triggers* and *coping mechanisms* that **Change** all the time the *ONE* thing that doesn't **Change** is I need to make sure I **Rest** when I need to **Rest**.

If I feel I'm getting tired and low then **Rest** is the thing that has to be done above pretty much anything else....

If I get the **Rest** I need things plod along just fine....

If I don't get the **Rest** I need then sooner or later the poops going to hit the fan and we will be going on yet another journey to Dolallytapsville....

S - Stigma

Stigma.... Fuck *Stigma*!!!!

Stigma will always exist, get over it....

That's *Stigma* covered, now on to T....

T - Time

As the saying goes: -

*"**Time** heals all wounds"*....

Yes very annoying when people say it to you but when you are able to say it to yourself then, then my friends you are getting somewhere.

When I had my mental breakdown in 2013 I remember *KNOWING* *"My life was over"* there was *NO* doubt in my mind that sooner or later I would *HAVE* to take my own life because there was no coming back from where I now found myself....

I now *KNOW* what absolute bullshit what I believed 100% back in 2013 was and it has only been possible with ***Time***....

Oh.... And....

- Lots of medication....

- Lots of ups and downs....

- Lots of horrendous episodes....

- Lots of thinking about killing myself....

- Lots of feeling like I'm banging my head against a brick wall....

- Lots of believing I was a waste of a human being….

- Lots of not being able to understand why life was worth living….

- Lots of time fighting off the **Demons** and their cruel taunts….

I think you probably get my point by now....

Added to those many negative things there has been an unwavering determination inside me not to let, whatever this **Illness** is *EVER* beat me! And a totally and utterly exhausting, at times, amount of effort day in day out, hour in hour out to keep fighting back and keep moving forward with my recovery.

All the negative stuff and all the positive stuff needs **Time** to work itself out and come to some sort of balance. If you trust me at all by now I can tell you no matter how bad things are at the moment *YOU CAN* get back on track.

I've spoken with and I'm proud to say I've helped people do this. Problem is I've spoken to many people who want things to *"be back on track NOW!"* I'm sorry if you want that to happen I've got to tell you recovering from Mental Illness, Addiction and Associated Issues doesn't and will never work like this. Exactly the same as in normal, everyday life, it's a struggle and you've got to be up for the fight if you want to make it out the other side.

Even if at the moment you don't want to make it out the other side, you will find a better place a stronger platform to build your recovery on and rebuild your life....

In order to get to a better place it takes *Time*....

I can tell you from my personal experiences and experiences of many other people i have spoken with that *Time* and effort is very much worth it!!!!

And again: -

If I can do this then YOU CAN TOO!!!!

U - Uncontrollable

I don't really like this word but I know I've said it thousands of times and I've heard it said thousands of times that: -

*"My world and **Illness** is **Uncontrollable**".*

This next sentence might shock you a bit, but....

Yes your **Illness**, your issues whatever they are are totally and utterly **Uncontrollable** and if what you are seeking is to be able to **Control** your Mental Illness, Addiction and Associated Issues I'm afraid your seeking the unachievable.

I did *say, "The next sentence might shock you".*

However.... That being said, does anyone ever really control anything 100%? Saying you are seeking the unachievable isn't a negative and defeatist thing to say because it's not just your issues that are **Uncontrollable** it's all life that is **Uncontrollable**.

We never know what's going to happen tomorrow, we can walk around a corner and bump into someone we haven't seen for a long time there's nothing we could of done to **Control** that. If we didn't happen to be walking around that corner obviously we wouldn't of bumped into that person, but here's the thing **decisions are nothing but 50/50 guesses** and whichever way we guess/decide we have to **Accept** it and own our guess/decision....

So.... Yes your life, your **Illness**, your issues may very well be **Uncontrollable** and they may always be **Uncontrollable**. But once you can **Accept** this, instead of wasting huge amounts of time and energy trying to **Control** your world you can start working on a way to start **MANAGING** your Mental Illness, Addiction and Associated Issues....

I could write pages and pages on the subject of *Managing* your Mental Illness, Addiction and Associated Issues, but I'm not going to. *I'm just going to ask you to stop trying to Control your world and start Managing it....*

The issues we have, be it Mental Illness, Addiction, Anxiety, Depression, Self Harm, PTSD, Eating Disorders any many many others are issues that will and can effect our lives negatively everyday.

Once you've **Accepted** whatever your **Illness** and issue is then your recovery can begin. *YOU* can keep moving forward with *YOUR* recovery. *YOU* have to stop *trying* to **Control** the **Uncontrollable** and *start Managing* whatever your **Illness** and issues throw at you that day or that hour, spot what's going on and find a way to *Manage* whatever it is into something much less painful, horrendous, damaging and negative. If the next day the world throws another bag of poop at us we simply have to start all over again *Managing* whatever's ducking us up today....

V - Vicious Circle

I know there's quite a few of you that will know exactly what I'm going to talk about here....

Whether your issue is Mental Illness, Addiction or Issues such as self-harm, eating disorders, PTSD etc you will all be aware of your own **Vicious Circle**....

Everything seems to be going along reasonably okay and then as has happened many many times before the seemingly inevitable happens and there's a whole new pile of poop heading your way that you're going to have to deal with and fight your way through. At first you will probably be thinking: -

*"I can't get through this again, this episode is the one that's going to finish me off, my life has been nothing but a **Vicious Circle** of one issue after another, one pile of poop after another, I just can't handle it again"....*

Well, if you're thinking that it's understandable but also a huge pile of....

BULLSHIT!!!! EVERY OTHER TIME THIS HAS HAPPENED YOU GOT THROUGH IT AND YOU'LL GET THROUGH AGAIN AND EVERY SINGLE TIME IT HAPPENS IN THE FUTURE....

THAT'S A 100% SUCCESS RATE.... FACT!!!!

The thing is this **Vicious Circle** phenomenon isn't just part of life for us mentalists, addicts, self harmers or those of us that have many other issues it's part of everyone's life, I would sum it up simply as *"ship hattens"*.

In normal life you can be plodding along nicely without a care in the world, and then, out of nowhere and just like in our lives, us with the *"issues"* those without our *"issues"* the seemingly inevitable happens....

Here is a made up example of what might happen....

You've had an expensive weekend celebrating someone's wedding or significant birthday, you know one of those extra expenses that you can justify because it's a special occasion, besides which you get paid on Thursday. It'll be ok to skirt around Overdraft City for a couple of days as long as you don't get any unexpected expenses....

And then....

You get a puncture on the way to work; your spare tyre is bald because you forgot to get it done the last time you had to change a wheel. The puncture on this tyre isn't fixable because the nail is in the sidewall and now you've got to spend £70 you just haven't got on a new tyre. If you are rational and issue free you might just think, *"I've got that £80 I've been saving for a rainy day"* or *"I'll have to ask the family for a small short term loan"*. You will get it sorted and be on your way.

It doesn't tend to work like this for those of us with *issues*. Yes if we're in a good place we will simply deal with it like a *normal* would....

Or....

It could be that straw that breaks the camels back and pushes us over the edge and possibly into a downward spiral, just like what's happened many times before we are back in that **Vicious Circle** we've been in again and again and again. Our survival or our continued recovery is now threatened and the way we chose to react now can ruin the next couple of hours or days of our life, back where our issues have us pinned down and no use to the world.

Often we will react in the negative way we've always reacted in, so strap in; the next couple of days could be a bumpy ride. Or we can find some strength to break our usual **Bad learned behaviour**. We can step ahead of the thing that's possibly taking us back into our **Vicious Circle** and say, *"it is what it is"* or *"ship hattens"* and find a practical and effective way to react to avoid jumping back into our **Vicious Circle**.

I believe, *very unfortunately*, there are times when we just can't react in a better way and when this happens we just have to *"ride it out"* the best we can until we pick ourselves back up. One of the #'s

I use on social media all the time is, **#PickYourBattles**, sometimes you have to realise for yourself this is a battle you can either win now or maybe it's a battle that you just can't fight at this time.

You need *Rest* and to recharge so you can come back fighting hard. This is what we've done again and again and again and what we will continue to do again and again and again because we are *WARRIORS!*

Whatever life throws at us we can beat it maybe not today, maybe not tomorrow but when we have *Rested* and recharged we will be back to kick our *Demons* butt again and again and again….

We can chose to keep believing our life is a *Vicious Circle* or we can *Accept* *"ship hattens"* in everyone's life that they have to cope with or at times can't cope with.

Breaking away from the *Vicious Circle* phenomenon is difficult but if you can do it, it is very powerful and yet another example of reprogramming our noggins to react in a different way, another example of spotting *our Bad Learned Behaviours* and actively working on *Changing* them for the better.

W - Why?

I've spoken about **Why?** soooooooo many times I don't know how to start this one.... So I'm going to start with a **Question** and a personal statement....

Question - **Why** bother with **Why?...**

Personal Statement - I gave up the **Question** **"Why?"** a long time ago....

So what do I say now?...

The basic premise of the **Question** and personal statement is that a long time ago I realised the **Question Why?** is an utter waste of time and energy....

Don't get me wrong I've spent most of my life asking many **Why? Questions**....

- "Why me?"

- "Why can't I get out of bed?"

- "Why am I an alcoholic/addict?"

- "Why has my life been such an horrendously painful journey?"

- "Why did I just burst into tears for no reason whatsoever?"

- "Why did I have to be born?"

- "Why am I mentally ill?"

- "Why did I have a mental breakdown?"

And many many other **Questions** along those lines, my guess is most of you will of asked those **Questions** and many others over and over again.

The thing is there is no actual answer to the **Questions Why?** Apart from simply *"Because"*. I know what you're thinking, *"that's bollox"* and if you are thinking that you are both right and wrong....

So this week I've been struggling, I sort of know **Why** I've been struggling but if I was still like I was before I stopped asking the **Question Why?** I would have analysed everything that's happened every day, every hour, every minute and in doing that I would have wasted a whole lot of time, effort and valuable energy trying to answer the **Question Why?**

Instead of wasting that energy on pointless **Questions** and over analysing everything. I've used that energy to help a few people, go to a few meetings, get out and get some fresh air and mindfully **Rest** to get back on my feet. And in using my energy in that more positive way I have gone from suicidal thoughts on Monday to *"I'm gunna take over the world"* on Friday. *(Taking over the world may seem a little over the top but remember,* *this life we live actually has no limits so why not aim for the big things and believe that you can take over the world....).*

I think it's definitely worth adding once I'd decided not to bother with the **Why? Question** for when I'm struggling or having an episode eventually I realised it was also pointless asking **Why?** when I was doing ok.

This came from one day when I felt I was in a really good mood and instead of just enjoying and making the most of the good mood I was in, I got concerned I was only feeling that way because I was manic. Thinking like this destroyed my good mood instantly and put me on the back foot again, now instead of the usual fighting against a low mood I was for some reason fighting against a good mood that might be due to mania but could just be simply a good mood. What a total and utter waste of what could be a good opportunity to **"enjoy the good"** mood and make some happy memories to help me cope better, *Manage* better in the future.

Fairly recently I was introduced to crystals, grounding and I had a Reiki treatment. I was very surprised that I was now grounding most mornings, basically standing bare foot in the back garden breathing deeply with my eyes closed whilst clutching one of my currently three different crystals. I didn't believe any of this airy-fairy malarkey would do anything to help all that stuffs for the hippie's right? Well I can tell you it has made a difference to my life and if we go right back to the start of this a to z and the word *Acceptance* that's all I did and all I do, I just *Accept* stuff for what it is. Be it spiritual stuff that I don't understand or just *Accepting* today isn't that good because I feel low or I'm in a good mood lets *Accept* that and make the most of it. And in *Accepting* all this stuff I don't waste any time asking *Why?*

There could be one reason, there could be hundreds of reasons but wasting energy on working out what that one reason is or what those hundreds of reason could be.... Nah, not for me and I hope you will be able to do the same because if you trust me at all by now taking this approach yourself will make a huge difference....

Don't ask *Why?*

Just *Accept* the good or bad and react accordingly....

Simple as that....

X - erm....

I wonder how many of you have thought about this as you've gone through this a to z guide so far *"I can't wait to see what word he comes up with for X"*.

I could do the obvious tortured reference to *exboozehound*, eg, *Xboozehound*, but that would drive me insane. I get rather upset when anyone else spells exboozehound any other way than how its tattooed on my chest, all lower case and italics so the previous exboozehound's in this sentence have already annoyed me a little so let's do it right.... *exboozehound*.... Ooh that feels better already....

No, I have another plan for *X* and that plan is basically find interesting *X* words, in particular positive *X* words. Of course I'm going to ask the font of all knowledge that's worth knowing for these *X* words.... Yup, Google....

So....

X - Xenagogue (plural xenagogues)

One who conducts strangers; a guide. So **Xenagogy**, conduction of strangers: used as the title of a guidebook.

Used in a sentence in 1570-6 by Lombard....

*"The places, whereof I meant to make note in this my **Xenagogue** and perambulation of Kent."*

Now that all makes perfect sense now doesn't it????

(I'm going to have to Google Lambarde now, and so are you….)

Y - You

This could be the most important tool in your toolbox of recovery tools, there's endless options for ways to deal with Mental Illness, Addiction and Associated Issues such as PTSD, Self Harm and Eating Disorders etc but when the poop hits the fan *ONLY YOU* can help *YOU*....

The people who I've spoken with and helped and others that I've seen getting onto a good, fairly stable recovery are those that put the effort in. Someone with thirty years experience of Mental Illness and everything that goes with that, including being sectioned many times, once said to me....

"I've met many people over the last 30 years trying to deal with mental illness and addiction etc but I don't think I've ever met anyone that puts as much hard work into their recovery as you do"....

It puzzled me a bit at first but when I thought about it I thought, *"He could well be right"*. **He usually is....**

I have worked very hard, picking myself up again and again and again and beating my **Demons** and the other things my Mental Illness does to me, what I deal with and indeed we all have to deal with is *NOT* easy to keep doing again and again and again.

Without a hell of a lot of effort from **YOU**, **YOU** simply will not start to learn how to *Manage* your issues whatever they are. It is very important that **YOU** make the distinction and **Accept** it's definitely not **Control** them but definitely **Manage** them.

I've seen so many people who get new medication, counselling, psychology, a psychiatrist, an appointment for talking therapies, CBT, Mindfulness etc etc all of a sudden seemingly believe their issues will now be **Fixed** by the professionals. Sorry but **NO-ONE** and **NOTHING** is going to **Fix YOU**, **YOU** have to work hard consistently to get any sort of recovery and maintain it.

I've also seen so many people who get some new thing that's going to **Fix** them and when they realise that they are going to have to put some effort in themselves they just give up and fall back into their old **Bad Learned Behavioural** negative ways and patterns. It does not please me to say I have seen people *"just give up and fall back into their **Bad Learned Behavioural** negative ways and patterns"* and I hope I'm not upsetting people but unfortunately it's the truth....

Any recovery and stability can only work if YOU make it work. When the seemingly inevitable happens (the Vicious Circle from earlier) and everything falls apart again and let's be honest it will at some point only YOU can pick yourself back up again, have a word with yourself and start all over again. This is simply life, whether

YOU have an issue or not if you're going to move forward with YOUR life, YOU have to put in the hard work....

YOU!!!!"....

I promise YOU, YOU can do this and I promise the hard work and effort is definitely worth it....

And again: -

If I can do this then YOU can do it too!!!!

Z - Z's

I'm not going to say much on this, partly because I'm embarrassed that I've basically cheated with **Z** and gone for **Z's**....

In order to start **YOUR** recovery from whatever issues **YOU** have **YOU** are going to need sleep or **Z's.**

If **YOU** can't sleep then **Rest.**

If **YOU** can't sleep *(get some **Z's)** or **Rest** sufficiently then see your GP or psychiatrist and find a way to get sufficient sleep (**Z's**) and/or **Rest**.

Without sleep (**Z's**) or the ability to **Rest** calmly and mindfully **YOU** Managing **YOUR** Mental Illness, Addiction and Associated Issues is going to be a whole lot harder.

My sleep patterns have always been sporadic with or without the previous copious amounts of booze I used to tip down my throat. But I now have a sort of way to cope with this; there's no point in telling you how I cope with this as I believe this is an individual path we all have to find our own way. But take my word if you think you'll never be able to get proper sleep you are probably right if you're looking for the 8 hours a night. In my experience sometimes you need more than 8 hours and other times you don't, it's individual to you and what's happening in your life at this time....

Get some **Rest** and get some **Z's** and the task of navigating our world of Mental Illness, Addiction and Associated Issues gets just that little bit easier....

"enjoy the good and ride out the bad"

Keep going ;)

Jon aka *exboozehound*

Do you remember right back at the start in **Introduction 2** I told a short story and told you I had covered **A** for **Acceptance** and **B** for **Bad Learned Behaviours?**

Did you manage to **Accept** that I wasn't seemingly talking out of my butt and see that I had indeed covered **A** for **Acceptance** and **B** for **Bad Learned Behaviours?**

Here's the important part of the story again....

"After the gym I had a pork sandwich sitting by the clock in Halesowen outside a pub known locally as "Picks". A wasp wouldn't leave me alone, wasps don't bother me at all now, and this is because an ex-girlfriend was terrified of wasps. I had to do something about my fear of them, or we would never be able to sit outside in the sun eating lunch or just having a drink in the sun."

If you haven't worked it out, allow me....

Being afraid of wasps is a **Bad Learned Behaviour**, probably picked up subconsciously from seeing people running away screaming at them when you were a kid, unless you're actually allergic to the sting it's an irrational fear and a **Bad Learned Behaviour**.

Realising fearing wasps was irrational and in order to be able to do something I like doing, sitting in the sun, I had to **Accept** it was irrational and do something about it.

So you see that rubbish story did cover **A** for **Acceptance** and **B** for **Bad Learned Behaviours**.

Actually I've just realised the short story covered something else that I've mentioned a few times throughout this a to z guide, **Reprogramming and Rebuilding our Noggins**. I didn't just say to myself: -

"Right that's it I am no longer afraid of wasps"....

I had to work at it, just like I've had to work at my recovery, I had to **Reprogram and Rebuild my Noggin** not to fear them and slowly it became so....

Right that's if from me for now, Catch you soon

Lots of love

Jon Mansell aka *exboozehound*.

"enjoy the good and ride out the bad"

#MentallyIllNoShameWhatsoever

Printed in Great Britain
by Amazon

21794785R00057